Pulleys in Action

Gillian Gosman

PowerKiDS
press.

New York

Published in 2011 by The Rosen Publishing Group, Inc.
29 East 21st Street, New York, NY 10010

First Edition

Editor: Maggie Murphy
Book Design: Kate Laczynski
Photo Researcher: Jessica Gerweck

Photo Credits: Cover, p. 1 © www.istockphoto.com/Jim Kruger; back cover and interior cement background graphic © www.istockphoto.com/walrusmail; Back cover and interior graphic (behind some images) © www.istockphoto.com/Ivan Gusev; pp. 4–5, 9–12, 15–17, 22 Shutterstock.com; p. 6 © www.istockphoto.com/René Lorenz; p. 7 Jeff J. Mitchell/Getty Images; p. 13 Daniel Acker/Bloomberg via Getty Images; p. 14 De Agostini/Getty Images; p. 18 © www.istockphoto.com/lamiel; p. 19 Rolf Sjogren/Getty Images; pp. 20–21 © Rosen Publishing.

Library of Congress Cataloging-in-Publication Data

Gosman, Gillian.
  Pulleys in action / Gillian Gosman.
      p. cm. — (Simple machines at work)
  Includes index.
  ISBN 978-1-4488-0681-2 (library binding) — ISBN 978-1-4488-1294-3 (pbk.) — ISBN 978-1-4488-1295-0 (6-pack)
  1. Pulleys—Juvenile literature. I. Title.
  TJ1103.G68 2011
  621.8'11—dc22
                        2009053019

Manufactured in the United States of America

CPSIA Compliance Information: Batch #WS10PK: For Further Information contact Rosen Publishing, New York, New York at 1-800-237-9932

Contents

What Is a Pulley?

Pulleys are all around you! They are at work on bikes, flagpoles, window shades, sailboats, and some elevators. Pulleys are at work in buildings, in factories, and on farms, too. These pulleys make it possible to raise and lower heavy **loads** with **ease**.

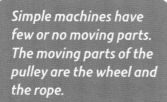

Simple machines have few or no moving parts. The moving parts of the pulley are the wheel and the rope.

A pulley is one of six common simple machines, or objects that do work. The other simple machines are the lever, the **inclined** plane, the wheel and axle, the screw, and the wedge. **Compound** machines, also called **complex** machines, are machines made up of many smaller simple machines. Tractors, cranes, and bulldozers are all compound machines.

A common place where pulleys are found is on ships and boats. For example, these pulleys are used on the sails of a sailboat.

The Parts of a Pulley

Here you can see two separate fixed pulleys, one beside the other. Each pulley has its own wheel with a rope looped around it.

A pulley is a wheel, also called a sheave or a drum. The wheel turns on an axle, or rod. It often has a groove, or path, along its outside. A rope, chain, or cable slides through the groove. Wheels and axles may be made out of wood, metal, or plastic. The wheel may be as small as a strawberry or as large as a car. What it is made of and how big it is depends on where and how it will be used.

The most basic pulley is a fixed pulley. It is called a fixed pulley because the axle of the wheel is fixed, or stuck in place. There are also movable pulleys, which have loose axles. Compound pulleys are systems of two or more pulleys that work together.

Here, a movable pulley lowers a submarine into the water. The submarine is attached to the bottom of the pulley by long ropes.

A Pulley's Work

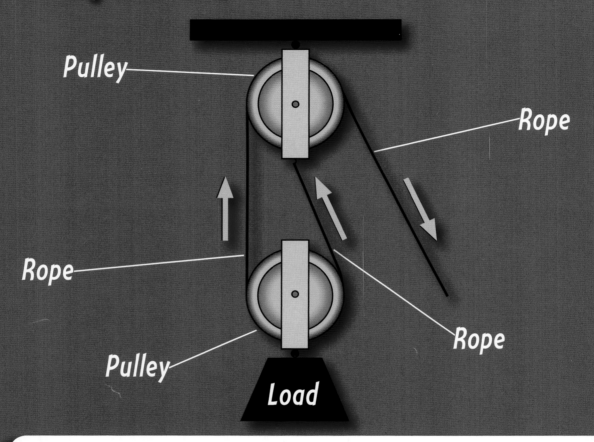

Pulley

Rope

Rope

Rope

Pulley

Load

Pulleys do three kinds of work. Some pulleys are used to change the direction of the **force**, or the push or pull, on the machine. Other pulleys work with belts or **gears** to share force from one system to another. Finally, some pulleys are used to multiply, or increase, force in order to carry a great weight.

Mechanical advantage, or **leverage**, is the measure of how much a machine increases the force applied to, or used on, it. The higher the mechanical advantage, the less **effort** it takes to lift or lower a load with a pulley.

9

The Fixed Pulley

Pulling down on one end of the rope causes the other end of the rope, where the flag is clipped, to go up. That is how we raise the flag.

An example of a fixed pulley is the pulley used to raise a flag on a flagpole. A circle of rope runs through the pulley. We clip the flag to one side of the rope then pull down on the other side of the rope, raising the flag. The rope moves through the wheel's groove, but the wheel's axle never moves because it is fixed in place. The fixed pulley on a flagpole changes the direction of the force we apply from down to up.

A fixed pulley has a mechanical advantage of 1. This means that to lift the flag, you have to apply the same force to one end of the rope that the flag's weight applies to the other end.

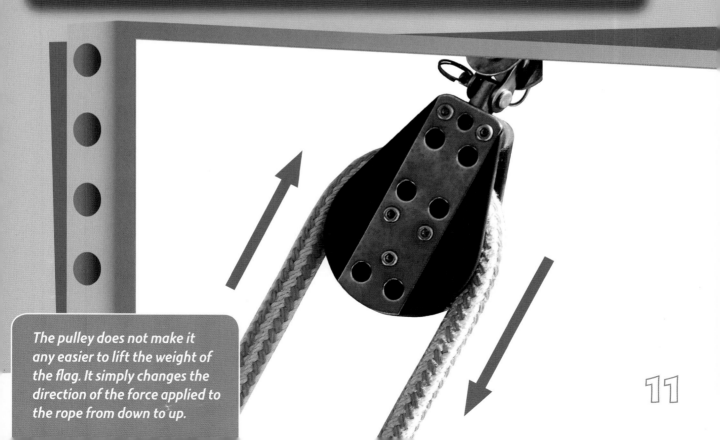

The pulley does not make it any easier to lift the weight of the flag. It simply changes the direction of the force applied to the rope from down to up.

Movable and Compound Pulleys

The mechanical advantage of a compound pulley, such as this one, depends on the number of pulleys working together and how many times the rope is looped between them.

A movable pulley is one with a loose, or free, axle. This kind of axle can move up, down, and side-to-side in space. On a movable pulley, one end of the rope that runs through the groove of the wheel is often fixed. The load is attached directly to the wheel, rather than to the rope, like on a fixed pulley. This means that the wheel moves with the load.

Fixed and movable pulleys may be used together, with the rope running through one wheel and then another. A system of two or more pulleys working together in this way is called a compound pulley. Compound pulleys make it even easier to lift heavy loads.

This man is using a movable pulley. A movable pulley has a mechanical advantage of 2. It doubles the force applied to the machine.

The First Pulley

This is a portrait of Archimedes. Archimedes is also known for his inventions that used other simple machines, including the lever and the screw.

ARCHIMEDE de Syracuse
Mathematicien né 550 ans avant
Jesus-Christ.

The first block and tackle pulley was designed by a Greek **mathematician** and **inventor** over 2,000 years ago. The mathematician's name was Archimedes. Archimedes lived in Sicily, an island that is part of present-day Italy. He invented many tools for use in work, war, and everyday life. Perhaps none was so useful to the sailors and fishermen of the Mediterranean Sea as the block and tackle.

A block is a set of wheels joined by one axle. One fixed block and one movable block are tackled, or joined together by rope. Used together, the blocks can lift whole boats in and out of the water. They can also raise and lower a ship's sails.

Pulleys make it easy for people to raise and lower sails on sailboats and ships. Like the pulley on a flagpole, the pulleys on boats change the direction of the force applied to the rope. The sail rises when the rope is pulled down.

Pulleys Today

Pulleys are used in almost every **industry**. We need them to make, move, build, and fix the goods we buy, the buildings around us, and the roads, bridges, and tunnels on which we travel.

Cranes, large and small, are used around the world. Crawler cranes work on buildings and roads.

Floating cranes are used to build bridges and seaports. Aerial cranes carry loads to places that cannot be reached by road. In factories, on farms, and at seaports and airports, fixed cranes, gantry cranes, and jib cranes do all kinds of heavy lifting jobs. All of these cranes use pulleys, powered by motors, to multiply force and make the job easier.

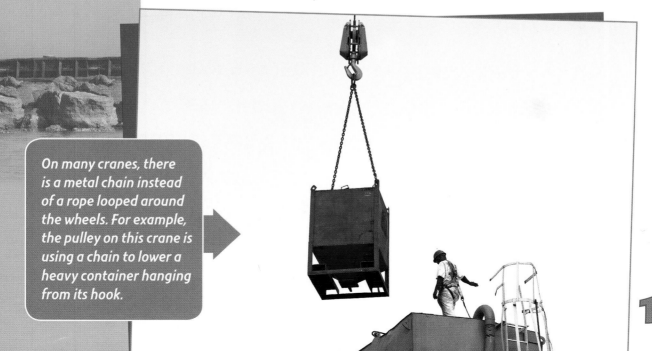

On many cranes, there is a metal chain instead of a rope looped around the wheels. For example, the pulley on this crane is using a chain to lower a heavy container hanging from its hook.

17

Pulleys and You

The pulley on a clothesline is fixed. This pulley changes the direction of the force so that the clothes move away from you when you pull the rope toward you.

If you look around your home, you may find pulleys at work! If you have window shades that raise and lower with the pull of a cord, then you have a pulley at work. The pulley in a window shade changes the direction of the force, so that when the cord is pulled down, the shade rises. If you have a clothesline that moves between two fixed wheels, you have pulleys at work. Pulleys in clotheslines also change the direction of the force.

Pulleys have been used in homes for many years. Common household objects from the past that used pulleys include water wells and hay-loft hooks, which can still be found in old homes and farms.

The pulley in a window shade makes it easy to raise and lower the shade so that a room can be made very dark or filled with sunlight!

19

An Experiment with Pulleys

*Have a friend help you do this simple **experiment** to learn more about pulleys.*

What You Will Need:
- *6 feet (2 m) of string*
- *a small object, such as a toy car*
- *a pencil*
- *an empty spool of thread or a napkin ring*
- *a friend*

1. Tie one end of the string to the car. Lift the car by pulling up on the string. Feel the resistance of the load, or how heavy the car feels when you lift it.

2. Put the pencil through the hole of the spool or napkin ring. The spool or napkin ring acts as the wheel and the pencil acts as its axis. Then run the string with the car tied to one end over the spool or ring. Keep hold of the loose end of the string.

3. Have a friend hold the pencil and spool at shoulder height. Now lift the car by pulling down on the string. The pulley is changing the direction of the force. As you pull down, the car is lifted up.

4. Experiment with more pulleys. You might make a block and tackle system by looping the string around a movable pulley and then around a second spool or ring on the pencil. Does the resistance of the load feel lighter now? Can you think of another compound pulley system?

step 3

Smooth Riding

The pulleys on a bicycle work a little differently. The two small gears and the chain that connects them make up the bicycle's pulley system. When you push down on a **pedal**, you are applying force to the front gear. The gear turns the chain, which turns the

back gear. When the back gear turns, the back wheel turns, too, pushing the bicycle forward.

Like the pulleys in a clothesline, bicycle gears are fixed pulleys that change the direction of the force. Unlike the pulleys in clotheslines, though, bicycle gears drive the wheels, pushing the bicycle forward.

complex (kom-PLEKS) Made up of many connected parts.

compound (KOM-pownd) Two or more things put together.

ease (EEZ) Comfort.

effort (EH-fert) The amount of force applied to an object.

experiment (ik-SPER-uh-ment) A test done on something to learn more about it.

force (FORS) Something that moves or pushes on something else.

gears (GEERZ) Wheels with teeth on the edge.

inclined (in-KLYND) Having a slope.

industry (IN-duh-stree) A business that makes something.

inventor (in-VEN-ter) Someone who makes something new.

leverage (LEH-veh-rij) The added help of using a machine to do work.

loads (LOHDZ) Things that must be carried or moved.

mathematician (math-muh-TIH-shun) A person who studies numbers.

pedal (PEH-dul) A tool that is pushed with a foot to make something work or move.

Web Sites

Due to the changing nature of Internet links, PowerKids Press has developed an online list of Web sites related to the subject of this book. This site is updated regularly. Please use this link to access the list:

www.powerkidslinks.com/sm/pull/